Usborne

Telling the Time
Activity book

Written by
Lara Bryan

Designed by
Sarah Vince, Katie Webb
and Jodie Smith

Illustrated by
Luana Rinaldo

butt

What is telling the time?

Time is the way we divide our day into seconds, minutes and hours.

It takes a second to hiccup.

Hic!

60 seconds make 1 minute.

It takes a minute to put on a coat.

60 minutes make 1 hour.

It takes an hour to make a cake.

Telling the time means reading the time from a clock. Most clocks look something like this.

There are two hands. The little hand points to the hours, and the big hand points to the minutes.

The hands always move in the same direction, known as clockwise.

The hours are shown by the big numbers on the clock face.

In this book, the little hand is always red and the big hand is always blue.

The minutes are shown by the gaps between the big numbers. There are five minutes between each.

It's 1 o'clock – time for lunch!

How to use this book

This book is split into four parts.

In the first and second parts, you'll find out about different kinds of clocks.

In the third and fourth parts, there are tips for working with lengths of time.

Telling the time:
pages 4 – 21

Discover how to read clocks and use a.m. and p.m.

Digital clocks:
pages 22 – 31

Find out how to use digital clocks, and about 24-hour time.

Lengths of time:
pages 32 – 45

Learn about small and big lengths of time, and how to use timelines.

More time:
pages 46 – 57

Find out about how time works around the world, and get lots of extra practice.

Look for Quick Quizzes throughout the book, to check what you've learned so far.

Give yourself a star from the sticker pages for each quiz you complete.

Turn to the answer pages at the back to check your answers or if you get stuck.

On the hour

When the big hand points to 12, the little hand tells you what hour it is.

It is 5 o'clock.

When it is exactly on the hour, it is called *o'clock*.

In between the hours, the big hand goes once around the clock face, and the little hand moves from one number to the next.

Now, it's 6 o'clock.

One hour (or sixty minutes) later...

7 o'clock. Time to wake up!

Look at the clock in each picture and fill in the time.

Wake up at .... o'clock.

Go to the workshop at .... o'clock.

Start building a new invention at .... o'clock.

By .... o'clock it is finished.

What times do these new clocks show?

.... o'clock   .... o'clock   .... o'clock

The experiments need to be checked at the times below. Draw the hands on the clocks.

Everlasting bubbles: 1 o'clock

Hot-and-cold ice cream: 10 o'clock

The inventor is testing his time machine. Fill in the times just above the clocks.

Time Machine

Departure time

Arrival time

....

....

Morning or night?

To make it clear if a time is in the morning, you can add 'a.m.' after it.

It's 10 a.m.

If a time is in the afternoon or at night, you can add 'p.m.'

It's 10 p.m.

To find out more, go to page 18.

Half past the hour

When the big hand is pointing down to six, and the little hand is halfway to the next hour, it is *half past* the hour.

So this clock says half past eight.

Half an hour is the same as 30 minutes. In 30 minutes it will be...

9 o'clock – time for superhero training!

SUPERHERO TRAINING

Look at this timetable, then match the right lesson kit from the sticker pages to each clock.

TIMETABLE

Half past nine	Flying
Half past ten	Invisibility
Half past eleven	Flame throwing

MIND CONTROL

This superhero can move clock hands with her mind. On each clock, draw the time she is thinking of.

Half past ten

Half past five

Half past two

Jet pack

Invisibility potion

FLYING

This superhero is flying in an around-the-world race. Look at the local time on each clock to complete the caption in the photo.

Moscow at ....

Mumbai at ....

Sydney at ....

MYSTERY SOLVING

A famous diamond was stolen at *half past two* today. To find the thief, this superhero needs to work out who was in the building then.

I arrived at one o'clock and left 30 minutes later.

Suspect A

Suspect A left the building at ....

I arrived at half past one and left half an hour later.

Suspect B

Suspect B left at ....

I arrived at two o'clock and left an hour later.

Suspect C

Suspect C left at ....

So the thief was ....

Draw the times onto the blank clocks, to show when each plant will be watered.

Half past eleven

Rainbow palms

Friendly creeper

Six o'clock

BUG WORKSHOP

Three o'clock

Can you finish the sign below? In summer, the greenhouse opens 30 minutes earlier and closes half an hour later.

OPENING TIMES

WINTER

Opens at: 10 o'clock

Closes at: 4 o'clock

SUMMER

Opens at: half 9

Closes at: .... past ....

Half past eight

Peeping poppies

8

Giant bamboo

The giant bamboo is measured daily at:

BUTTERFLY FEEDING IS AT
Eleven o'clock
Twelve o'clock
Four o'clock

It's eleven o'clock – only .... minutes till the next Fanged Fern Talk.

FANGED FERN TALK IS AT
Half past 11
Half past 2

Half past four

Fanged ferns

Two o'clock

Blushing cacti

GREENHOUSE QUIZ

Look around the greenhouse and circle 'True' or 'False'.

1. The butterflies are fed twice a day.   True / False

2. There is a bug workshop at three o'clock.   True / False

3. The bamboo is measured every day   True / False
   at half past eleven.

4. Only two plants are watered   True / False
   on the hour.

Quarter past and quarter to

You can divide an hour into four quarters.

When the big hand points to 3,
it is quarter *past* the hour.

It's quarter past one.

When the big hand points to 9,
it is quarter *to* the next hour.

It's quarter to two.

Only 15 minutes till
everyone arrives.

A quarter of an hour
is 15 minutes long.

15 minutes later...

Happy Birthday!

Each batch of cupcakes came out of the oven
at a different time. Look at the clocks and
write 1st, 2nd or 3rd by each shelf.

Now, use the stickers to decorate the cupcakes.
Add cherries to the *quarter past* the hour cupcakes
and chocolate stars to the *quarter to* the hour ones.

10

Can you pop the balloons with *quarter to* the hour times by crossing them out?

How many balloons did you pop? ....

What time were these photos taken?

Taken at quarter.................................

Taken at quarter..................................

Taken at quarter..................................

Can you set the times on the clocks for these party games?

We'll play musical chairs at four o'clock...

...pin the tail on the donkey at quarter past four,

...and pass the parcel at quarter to five.

5 minute gaps

The numbers on the clock face are five minutes apart.

At 60, you start counting again.

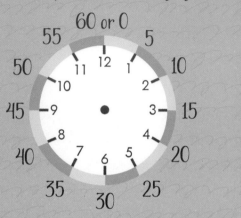

On the right-hand side, you count the minutes *past* the hour.

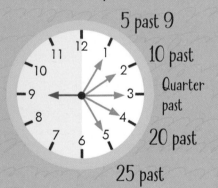

5 past 9

10 past

Quarter past

20 past

25 past

On the left-hand side, you count the minutes *to* the hour.

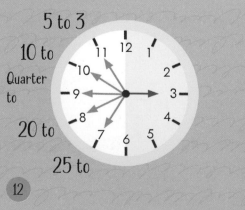

5 to 3

10 to

Quarter to

20 to

25 to

Fill in the times on these lesson posters.

LEARN TO SWIM

.... four

SYNCHRONIZED SWIMMING

.... five

Which race has just started? Look at the clock and circle one of the races below.

Race A: twenty-five to ten

Race B: twenty-five past ten

Race C: twenty to eleven

Draw the hands on each clock, so they match the time at the end of each slide.

1

2

3

4

Ten to three

Twenty to eleven

Twenty-five past six

Five past nine

Award each swimmer a rosette from the sticker pages, to show whether they came first, second or third.

FINISH TIMES

Half past three

Twenty-five to four

Twenty-five past three

A watch dropped in the pool at *five to five*, when it stopped working. Can you spot it in the lost property basket?

These aliens want to watch the sun set on different planets.
Match each alien to the planet with the right time.

Half past two

Twenty past four

Nine o'clock

Twenty-five to four

Five past eleven

Five to seven

Can you put these alien messages in the right order? Look at the time on the clocks and write 1 to 4 in the circles, with 1 being the earliest message and 4 the latest. Then read through all the messages in the right order.

CALL US TOMORROW AT 11 O'CLOCK AND

THANK YOU. FROM THE FRIENDLY ALIENS OF SG173

GREETINGS EARTHLINGS, ALTHOUGH YOU LOOK WEIRD, WE WANT TO BE FRIENDS

WE CAN HAVE A CHAT. GLAZUMPA, OR IN YOUR WORDS

Complete the activities on this page and the next, then make a clock following the instructions below.

Using the stickers, add twelve numbers to the clock face.

12
11
1
10
2
5 TO · PAST 3
8 6
7 4 9

1. Carefully tear or cut out this page.

2. Cut out the clock and the two hands along the dotted lines.

3. Choose which side you want to use as your clock face. Using a sharp pencil, poke a hole through the small circle on the clock face and hands. Then, push a paper fastener through all three and bend the ends back.

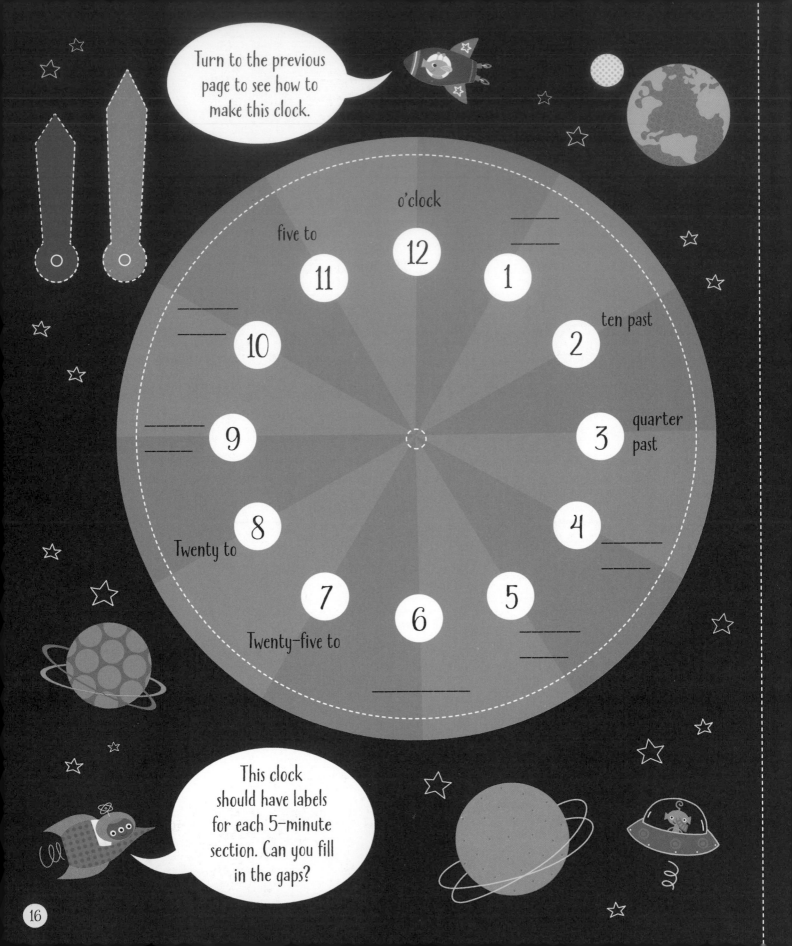

These rockets all have morning take off times. Shade them in following these clues.

- The first rocket to take off is blue.
- The green rocket takes off twenty minutes after the orange one.
- The red rocket leaves two hours after the first.

Half past nine   Ten o'clock   8 o'clock   Ten to ten

Check the clocks and fill in the missing times in this story.

At quarter .... eight on planet Zorb

I wish I had a flower.

At .... past ....

I'll go and find one.

At quarter .... ten

At quarter ....

I give up. Time to go home

At .... five, back on planet Zorb

Hurrah!

A.M. and P.M.

There are 24 hours in a day, but only 12 numbers on a clockface. To avoid confusion, times are split into a.m. and p.m.

9 o'clock in the *morning* is 9 a.m.

9 o'clock in the *evening* is 9 p.m.

a.m. stands for *ante meridiem*, which means 'before noon' or before midday in Latin.

p.m. stands for *post meridiem*, which means 'after noon' or after midday.

a.m. times run from midnight to noon...

12 noon

12 midnight

...and p.m. times from noon to midnight.

Write a.m. or p.m. by each time.

1. Half past six ....

2. Ten ....

3. Quarter past seven ....

4. Half past ten ....

These fireflies glow from 6 p.m. to 6 a.m.
Stick a glowing firefly by the times between those hours.

10 p.m.   4 p.m.   5 a.m.

12 midnight   8 p.m.   3 a.m.

18

These butterflies fly from 6 a.m. to 6 p.m. and the moths fly from 6 p.m. to 6 a.m. Can you give the butterflies bright patterns and leave the moths blank?

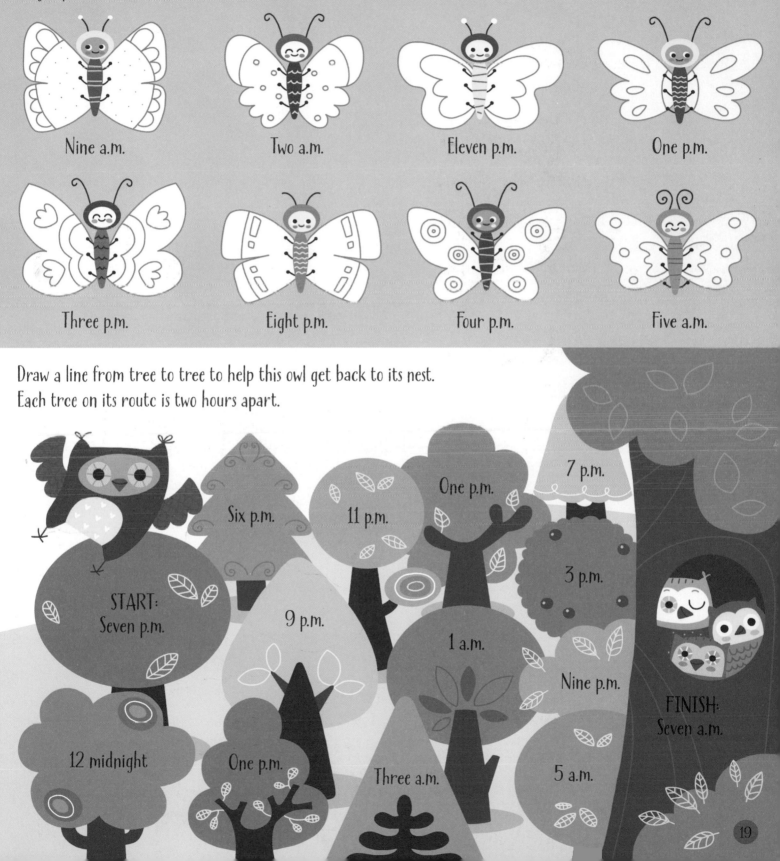

Nine a.m.

Two a.m.

Eleven p.m.

One p.m.

Three p.m.

Eight p.m.

Four p.m.

Five a.m.

Draw a line from tree to tree to help this owl get back to its nest.
Each tree on its route is two hours apart.

7 p.m.

Six p.m.

11 p.m.

One p.m.

3 p.m.

START:
Seven p.m.

9 p.m.

1 a.m.

Nine p.m.

FINISH:
Seven a.m.

12 midnight

One p.m.

Three a.m.

5 a.m.

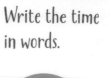

Draw the hands on the clocks.

Write the time in words.

Don't forget to check the answers at the back to add up your score or if you get stuck.

 Ten o'clock

 ....

 Five past eight

 ....

 Half past seven

 ....

 Quarter past one

....

Ten to seven

 ....

Score   Sticker

5

Score   Sticker

5

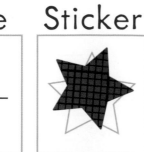

It's 10 a.m. Are these times 'earlier' or 'later' the same day?

P.M.

Earlier / later

A.M.

Earlier / later

A.M.

Earlier / later

P.M.

Earlier / later

Score

Sticker

_____
4

Draw lines between the matching times.

12 noon   12 at night

            11 in the
            morning

Midnight   Midday

            11 p.m.

                           11 in the
                           evening
11 a.m.

Put these times in order, from early to late, by writing a number in each circle.

Twelve midday   3 p.m.

6 p.m.   9 a.m.

11 a.m.   11 p.m.

Score

Sticker

_____
10

21

Digital clocks

Clocks with digital displays don't have hands. Instead, they show the time using numbers.

This side shows the hours → 11:40 ← This side shows the minutes

To read the time, you say the hours then the minutes.

It's eleven forty (which is the same as twenty to twelve).

If there is a zero in front of the hours, you *don't* read it out. If there is a zero in front of the minutes, you *do*.

It's nine fifty-five (or five to ten).

09:55

It's ten-oh-five (or five past ten). Time to play!

10:05

22

Fill in the missing digital times. Then, can you find a route to join up *all* the times in order, from early to late?

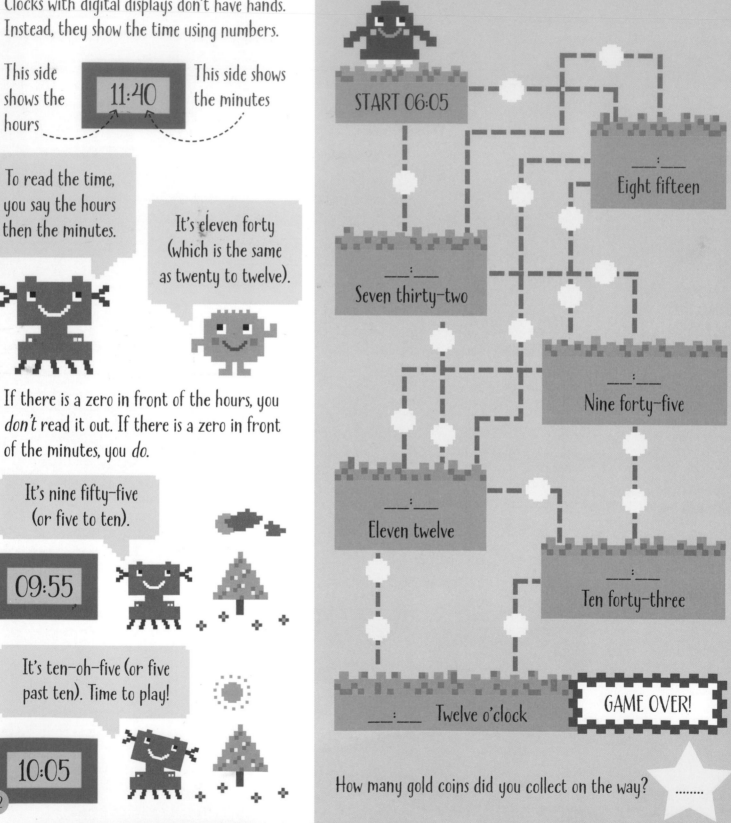

START 06:05

___:___ Eight fifteen

___:___ Seven thirty-two

___:___ Nine forty-five

___:___ Eleven twelve

___:___ Ten forty-three

___:___ Twelve o'clock

GAME OVER!

How many gold coins did you collect on the way? ....

The times by each creature show when it needs to be fed. Match each one to the food showing the same time.

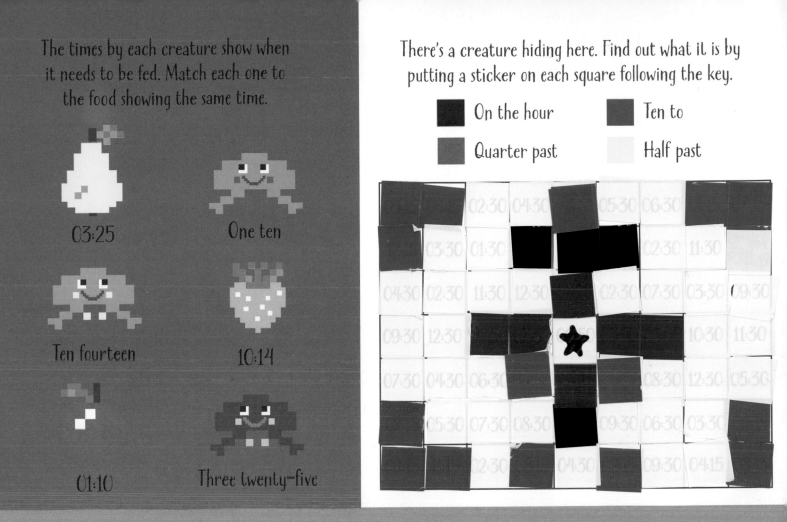

03:25

One ten

Ten fourteen

10:14

01:10

Three twenty-five

There's a creature hiding here. Find out what it is by putting a sticker on each square following the key.

On the hour   Ten to

Quarter past   Half past

Draw a line from clock to clock in intervals of ten minutes to help the time monster get through the maze.

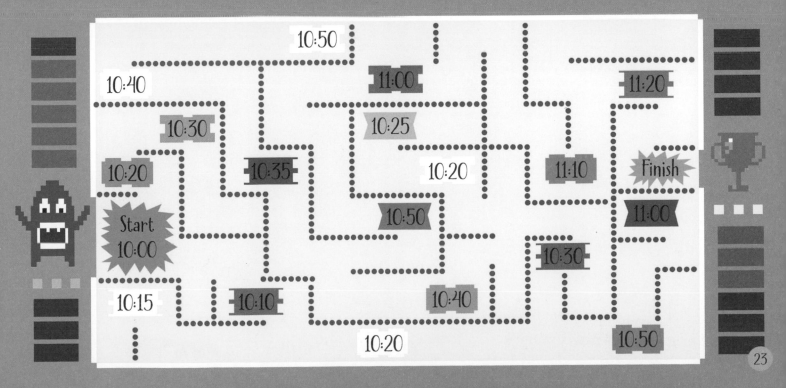

10:50

10:40

11:00

11:20

10:30

10:25

10:20

10:20

11:10

Finish

10:35

10:50

11:00

Start 10:00

10:30

10:15

10:10

10:40

10:20

10:50

Write 1st, 2nd or 3rd in each circle to show the order in which the guests arrive.

8:00 p.m.

7:40 p.m.

Ten to eight p.m.

It's quarter past eight now. Can you circle the activity that starts next in the chart below?

Write the times that these characters will be free from the spell and able to dance.

WISHES GRANTED
every hour on the hour

BANQUET
served at quarter
to nine p.m.

MAGIC CARPET RIDES
from 8:50 p.m.

I'll unfreeze at 8:30 p.m.
or .... past ....

At 9:40 p.m. or at
.... to ....
I'll be a handsome
prince again.

Write the time in numbers by each performer, to show when they will stop playing.

We'll play until half past ten.

___:___ p.m.

I'll stop at quarter to nine.

___:___ p.m.

I'll finish at eleven o'clock.

___:___ p.m.

Look at the time on the grandfather clock. Can you circle the dancer who is telling the *wrong* time?

It's nine fifty-five.

It's nine thirty-five.

It's five to ten.

Shade in the clocks showing *quarter to* times in red and those showing *quarter past* times in yellow.

8:15

11:15

5:45

Cinderella has to leave the ball at midnight. Cross out the two times that are wrong.

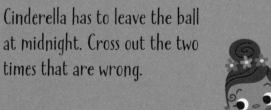

12 at night   Midday

12 noon   00:00

DIGITAL CLOCKS

24-hour time

Some digital clocks use '24-hour' time. This means that after midday the hours keep going up. So 1:00 p.m. becomes 13:00, and so on.

Because you count right through, you don't need a.m. or p.m.

To convert times after midday *into* 24-hour time, add 12 hours like this:

1:20 p.m.

$1 + 12 = 13$ → 13:20

To convert 24-hour times *back*, take away 12 hours:

17:40

$17 - 12 = 5$ → 5:40 p.m.

When it's on the hour, you can say 'hundred hours' instead of 'o'clock'. So 17:00 is 17 hundred hours.

When it's past the hour, you read the numbers as they appear. So 14:20 is 'fourteen twenty'.

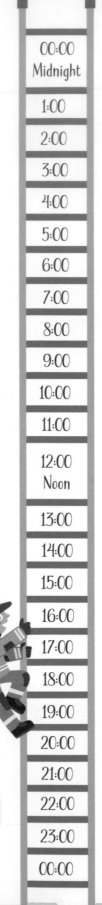

00:00 Midnight	
1:00	
2:00	
3:00	
4:00	
5:00	
6:00	
7:00	
8:00	
9:00	
10:00	
11:00	
12:00 Noon	
13:00	
14:00	
15:00	
16:00	
17:00	
18:00	
19:00	
20:00	
21:00	
22:00	
23:00	
00:00	

It's the fire station open day. Look at the timetable, then write the time in each picture.

Trying on uniforms	fourteen twenty
Sliding down the pole	fourteen fifty
Riding in the truck	fifteen hundred hours
Hose demonstration	fifteen thirty

This firefighter needs to get up for a night shift at quarter to eleven p.m. Add the alarm clock stickers showing the right time to the table.

Which of these hoses is spraying water?
Write its time using the 24-hour clock.

___ : ___

3rd
6:35 p.m.

2nd
11:47 p.m.

1st
4:12 p.m.

Convert the 24-hour times on the extinguishers into 12-hour times.

17:00

17 − 12 = ___ : ___ p.m.

___ : ___ p.m.

19:20

21:00

___ : ___ p.m.

Look at the clues below, then stick the names of the trucks onto the pictures.

'Roadstar' left at three p.m.   'Champion' left at ten p.m.   'Hero' left at one p.m.

13:00

15:00

22:00

FIRE FIRE

FIRE FIRE

FIRE FIRE

ROADSTAR

CHAMPION

HERO

It's 15:50.
Circle the bird who
has got the time wrong.

Ten to
three

Fifteen fifty

Ten to four

Three
fifty p.m.

This scientist uses 24-hour time in her notes.
Can you convert the times for her?

Find a leaf sticker with the matching
12-hour time to stick opposite each leaf.

ANIMALS SEEN TODAY

Iguana
2:15 p.m.
___:___

Millipede
5:55 p.m.
___:___

Tree frog
11:30 p.m.
___:___

Stag beetle
6:03 p.m.
___:___

16:00

4 p.m.

13:00

1 p.m.

20:00

8 p.m.

Colour in the birds using the key on the right. Tip: convert the times in the key to 24-hour time first.

7 p.m.
__:__

4 p.m.
__:__

8 p.m.
__:__

6 p.m.
__:__

1 p.m.
__:__

11 p.m.
__:__

3 p.m.
__:__

10 p.m.
__:__

Spot which bird these feathers belongs to.

Can you fill in the displays on these digital clocks using 12-hour time?

__ __ : __ __   Three ten

__ __ : __ __   Two thirty

__ __ : __ __   One o'clock

__ __ : __ __   Eleven fifty-five

__ __ : __ __   Ten to six

__ __ : __ __   Four twenty

Score

_____
6

Sticker

Finish writing out these times in words.

1. 07:15   seven ....

2. 05:55   .... to six

3. 11:20   eleven ....

4. 4:05   .... past four

5. 9:30   nine ....

Score

_____
5

Sticker

Try to fill in the times on these clocks using 24-hour time.

___:___   Ten p.m.

___:___   6:30 p.m.

___:___   Three fifty-five p.m.

___:___   Quarter to one p.m.

___:___   8:20 p.m.

___:___   Half past four p.m.

___:___   12:10 p.m.

Score

7

Sticker

Convert these 24-hour times into 12-hour times.

20:00   ___:___ p.m.

17:15   ___:___ p.m.

14:30   ___:___ p.m.

23:55   ___:___ p.m.

00:10   ___:___ a.m.

15:40   ___:___ p.m.

16:45   ___:___ p.m.

Score

7

Sticker

Seconds, minutes, hours

As well as telling the time, seconds, minutes and hours can also describe how *long* things take.

It takes a second to hiccup...

Hic!

...a minute to tie shoelaces...

...and an hour to cook a stew.

There are 60 seconds in one minute and 60 minutes in one hour.

You can convert intervals of time like this:

70 seconds = 60 + 10 seconds
70 seconds = 1 minute 10 seconds

95 minutes = 60 + 35 minutes
95 minutes = 1 hour 35 minutes

POLAR QUIZ
Can you circle the right time?

It takes 5 seconds / 5 hours for a puffin to swallow a fish.

Orca whales can leap out the water for 2 seconds / 2 hours.

Polar bears sleep for 7 minutes / 7 hours a day.

A moose spends 5 minutes / 5 hours a day grazing.

It takes a seal 30 seconds to catch a fish. Work out how many fish the seals can catch in the times below, then balance the right number of fish stickers on each seal's head.

Tip: 30 seconds is half a minute.

1 minute

3 minutes

How long does this polar explorer take to get ready?

Getting dressed: 10 minutes

Having breakfast: 15 minutes

Planning the day: 40 minutes

10 + 15 + 40 = ... hour and .... minutes.

To win the race, this husky racer needs to finish in less than 2 hours. Add up the times to see if she succeeds.

START

25 mins

30 mins

35 mins

20 mins

FINISH

25 + 30 + 35 + 20 = ...

Draw a line between the matching race times to show which husky gets which prize.

45 minutes

2 hours

1 hour and 50 minutes

120 minutes

110 minutes

¾ of an hour

How long?

Sometimes it's easy to work out how long something took...

The cat started eating at 3 o'clock and finished at five past three.

03:00   03:05

The cat was eating for 5 minutes.

Sometimes it's harder – in which case, it can help to draw a timeline...

How long is the pet show on for?

Draw a line with the start and end times. Then split it up, to help count up the times.

+1 hour   +5 hours   +30 mins

11:00   12:00   5:00   5:30

So the pet show is: 1 hr + 5 hrs + 30 mins
= 6 ½ hours long.

Pet Show
11 – 5:30 p.m.

Which tortoise took longer to eat?

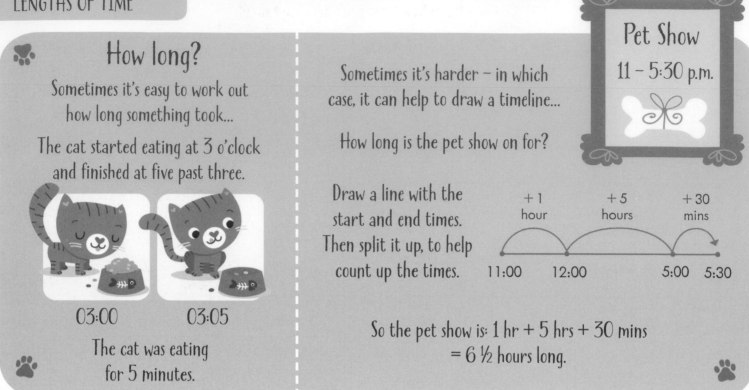

3:10

3:00

Zzz

4:05

3:45

Zzz

How long do the puppy events last altogether?

Tip: There are no gaps between the events, so you only need to work out 11:15 – 12:30.

11:15   12:15   12:30

1. 'Best puppy'
11:15 – 11:35

2. 'Waggiest tail'
11:35 – 12:00

3. 'Softest coat'
12:00 – 12:30

Can you fill in how long each activity takes?

Grooming: 11:00 – 11:30

.... minutes

Competing: 11:45 – 12:15

.... minutes

Prizegiving: 12:30 – 12:45

.... minutes

Which is the longest event?

Most playful kitten
15:00 – 15:40

Catch the mouse
15:45 – 16:30

Which pet had the longest journey home from the pet show?

17:20 – 19:30

18:45 – 20:50

You can use the timelines to help you work it out.

17:20   18:00   19:00   19:30   18:45   19:00   20:00   20:50

Start and end times

Timelines can be helpful when working out start and end times, too.

The train left at eight thirty in the morning, and arrived two and a half hours later. At what time did it arrive?

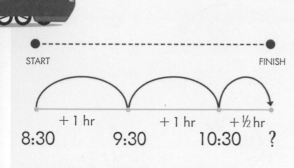

START   FINISH

+ 1 hr   + 1 hr   + ½ hr

8:30   9:30   10:30   ?

The train arrived at 11 a.m.

The bus arrived at eight a.m. after a 1 hour 10 minute journey. When did it set off?

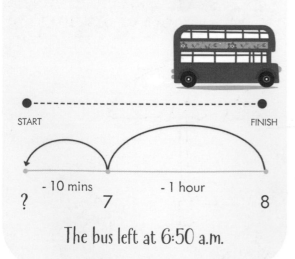

START   FINISH

- 10 mins   - 1 hour

?   7   8

The bus left at 6:50 a.m.

Each of these balloons spends forty minutes in the air. Draw the landing time for each one on its clock.

I took off at 9:00.

We took off at 10:10.

We took off at 11:30.

There is a helicopter ride every thirty minutes. Can you write the next times in the box?

NEXT RIDE

12:50

13:20

___:___

___:___

___:___

The green jet drops a parachutist at 14:05 and the red one at 15:45. Can you find the right point on each trail? Then, stick a parachutist from the sticker pages onto it.

13:15

+ 10 mins

+ 10

+ 10

+ 10

+ 10

+ 10

+ 10

+ 10

14:00

+ 15 mins

+ 15

+ 15

+ 15

+ 15

+ 15

+ 15

Can you work out when each pilot took off and write it on the plane?

This is a 30 minute flight and I'm landing at 14:15.

This is a 1 hour 30 minute flight. I'm landing at 15:45.

The air show starts at 11:30. Look at the weather forecast below, then work out if these spectators need sun hats or rain hats, and give them the right stickers.

One and a half hours after the start

Two and a half hours after the start

WEATHER FORECAST

12:00

13:00

14:00

37

Draw the route from the start to the cinema, adding up the times along the way. How long does the journey take?

....

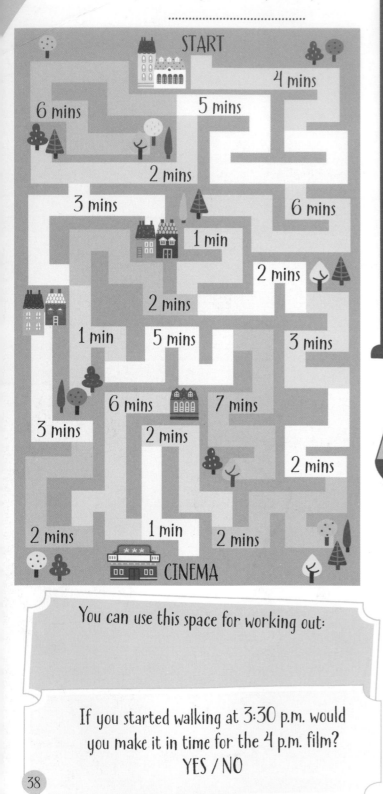

Add up the times in seconds on the popcorn cups to find out how long it took to make each batch.

$20 + 30 + 10 + 40$

This batch took

.... sec = ... min .... sec

$30 + 30 + 40 + 50$

This batch took

.... sec = ... min .... sec

Add the right ice cream scoops from the sticker pages, so that each cone adds up to one minute.

You can use this space for working out:

If you started walking at 3:30 p.m. would you make it in time for the 4 p.m. film?
YES / NO

= 10 sec   = 30 sec

= 20 sec   = 40 sec

THE INVENTOR 16:00-18:00

ONCE UPON A TIME... 19:00-20:45

JUNGLE JOURNEY 21:15-22:45

How long does each of the films below last in minutes?

.... minutes   .... minutes   .... minutes

BOO!

Running time: 1 ½ hours

A DOG'S LIFE

Running time: 2 hours

SUPERKIDS

Running time: 2 ½ hours

TICKETS

Film starts: 18:00

The film lasts for 90 minutes. When will it finish?

It'll end at ___:___

LENGTHS OF TIME

Days, weeks, months

There are other ways of counting larger lengths of time.

Days are 24 hours long, and officially start and end at midnight (or 00:00).

There are 7 days in a week.

There are about 30 days in a month and 12 months in a year.

February usually has 28 days, but it has 29 days in a 'leap year'. Turn to page 46 to find out more.

The exact number of days in a month varies:

January	31	July	31
February	28/29	August	31
March	31	September	30
April	30	October	31
May	31	November	30
June	30	December	31

Add a pirate flag sticker to the ship that will be away for the longest amount of time.

We're at sea for all of November and December.

We're at sea for all of December and January.

These pirates were born in the same year. Shade in their tops so the youngest is wearing a green top, the next youngest an orange top and the oldest a blue top.

I'm Cutlass Kate and I was born on the 10th of June.

My birthday is a week before Kate's.

My birthday is on the last day of May.

Work out how many days and weeks it will take the captain to reach Treasure Island.

.... days = ... weeks

1 day

1 day

3 days

2 days rest

5 days

7 days

2 days rest

Treasure Island

Solve the clues to find the column and row where the treasure is buried. Then, put a cross on the right square.

For the column you seek
How many days in a week?
Count this number across
And you won't get lost.

Then go up to the letter
Of the last month of the year
And then you will know
That the treasure is here!

A B C D E F G H I J

1 2 3 4 5 6 7 8 9 10

Counting years

A year is divided into 12 months, or 52 weeks, or 365 days (except in a leap year when it's 366, see page 46).

Some numbers of years have special names.

Decade = 10 years
Century = 100 years
Millennium = 1000 years

Can you write the correct age on each squirrel's acorn?

I'm half a decade old.

I'm Pip and I'm a decade old.

I'm three years older than Pip.

The baby deer is 40 weeks old. How many weeks till its first birthday?

Calendars

Calendars keep track of the days, weeks and months in a year.

A page in a calendar usually looks something like this...

Month   Days of the week

June						
Mon	Tues	Wed	Thur	Fri	Sat	Sun
			1	2	3	4
5	6	7	8	9	10	11
12	13	14	15	16	17	18
19	20	21	22	23	24	25
26	27	28	29	30		

This is Thursday 29th June.

The name of the month goes at the top. The columns show you the days of the week and the numbers tell you the date.

.... weeks

Can you mark the days of these events on the calendar, using the stickers from the sticker pages?

There's an archery contest on the last day of the month.

My birthday's on the third Wednesday.

The spring festival is on the 4th.

Can you write the day of the month at each journey checkpoint?

43

Choose the right unit of time to complete each sentence.

seconds – minutes – hours – days – months – weeks – years

A year is 365 or 366 ....

There are 7 days in a ....

There are 60 seconds in a ....

A month is 30 or 31 ....

1 hour is 60 ....

30 minutes is ½ an ....

A year is the same as 12 ....

There are 24 hours in a ....

A year is the same as 52 ....

Score

9

Sticker

Can you fill in the blanks?

3 weeks = ... days

a quarter hour = ... minutes

24 months = ... years

2 minutes = ... seconds

14 days = ... weeks

120 minutes = ... hours

1½ hours = ... minutes

90 seconds = ... minutes

30 minutes = ... hour

180 seconds = ... minutes

Score

10

Sticker

Can you fill in the blanks on these journey timelines?

Journey time: 1 hour 15 minutes

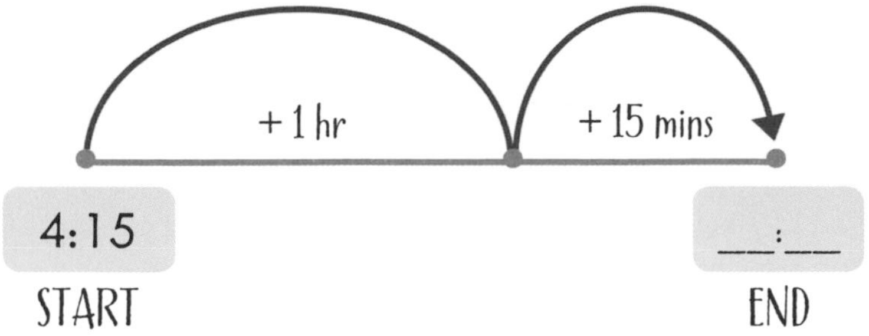

+ 1 hr   + 15 mins

4:15
START

___:___
END

Journey time: 2 hours

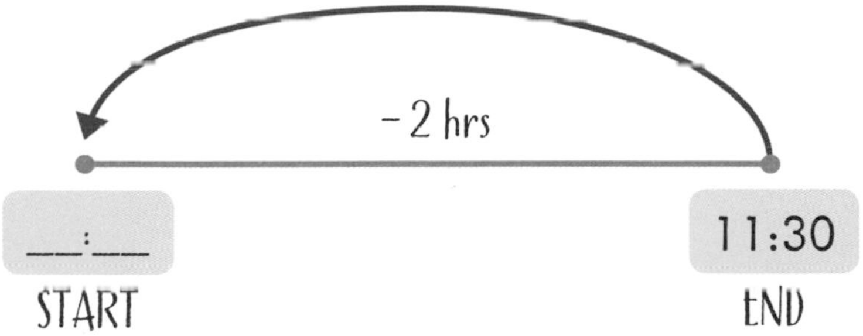

− 2 hrs

___:___
START

11:30
END

Journey time: ....

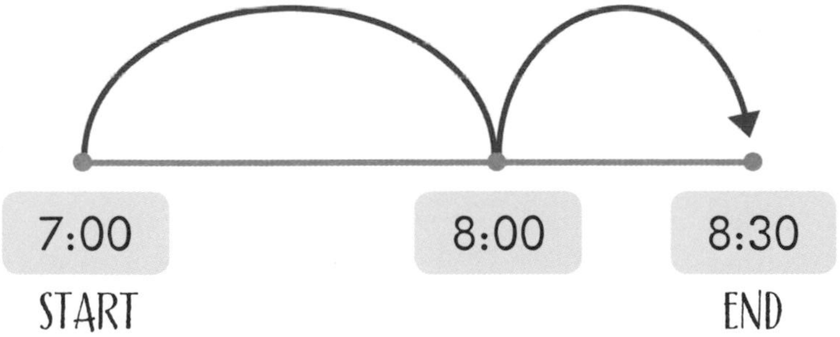

7:00
START

8:00

8:30
END

Score

3

Sticker

Can you fill in the blanks?

Journey times		
Start	End	How long it took
9:00	9:30	
4:30		1 hr 15 mins
	2:00	30 mins
11:15	13:15	
	17:20	30 mins
	19:45	1 hr

Score

6

Sticker

The Earth is constantly turning, like a spinning top. A day – or 24 hours – is the time it takes the Earth to spin around once.

It's light on the side that's facing the sun...

...and night on the other side, where it's dark.

Midday is in the middle of the daylight hours, when the sun is closest to that part of the Earth.

The Earth also travels around, or orbits, the sun. A year – or roughly 365 days – is the time it takes for the Earth to complete one orbit.

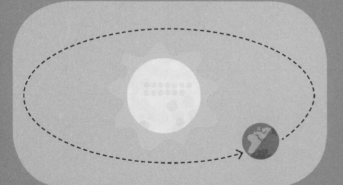

One orbit actually takes just *over* 365 days. So to catch up, every four years we add an extra day to February – making a 'leap year'.

How time works

The photos on the sticker pages were each taken at one of these spots on Earth. Look at the time of day on each photo and stick them by the right spot.

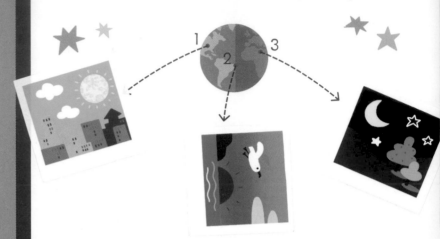

1 2 3

Can you match each turn to the number of hours it takes the Earth to complete it?

½ a turn	2 turns	1 turn
48 hours	24 hours	12 hours

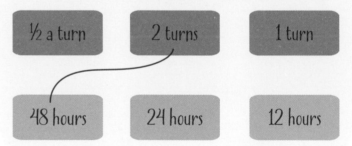

It was my birthday five days ago, how many days till the next one? (It's not a leap year.)

....

Can you circle true or false?

1. It takes the Earth 24 hours to turn around once.
TRUE / FALSE

2. It's night on the side of the Earth facing the sun.
TRUE / FALSE

3. It takes the Earth longer to orbit the sun on leap years.
TRUE / FALSE

4. The Earth is turning and moving around the sun at the same time.
TRUE / FALSE

Can you shade in the side of the Earth that is in shadow on each of these globes?

Every leap year's day, some astronomers have a party. They last had a party in 2016. Can you mark every following leap year in this calendar with a cake sticker?

LEAP YEAR PARTIES

February 29th 2016	
February 29th 2017	
February 29th 2018	
February 29th 2019	
February 29th 2020	
February 29th 2021	
February 29th 2022	
February 29th 2023	
February 29th 2024	
February 29th 2025	
February 29th 2026	
February 29th 2027	
February 29th 2028	

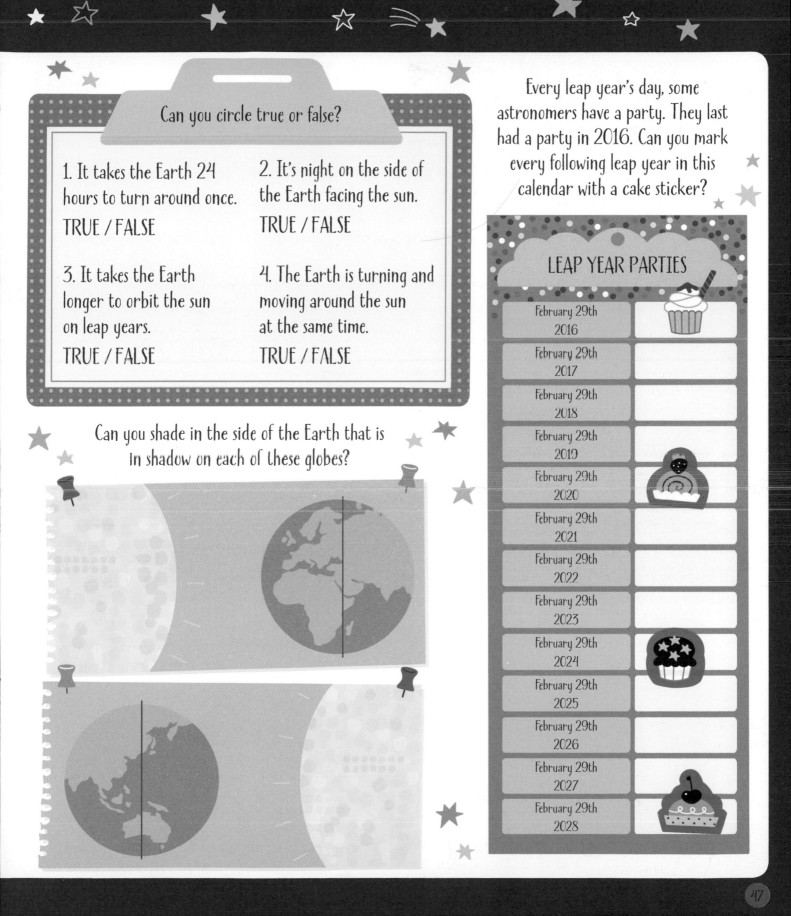

Time zones

The world is divided into 24 'time zones'. All the clocks in a time zone are set to the same time. When you move to a new time zone, the time changes. This map shows the different time zones around the world.

The zone in the middle is the standard time, from which time in other zones is calculated.

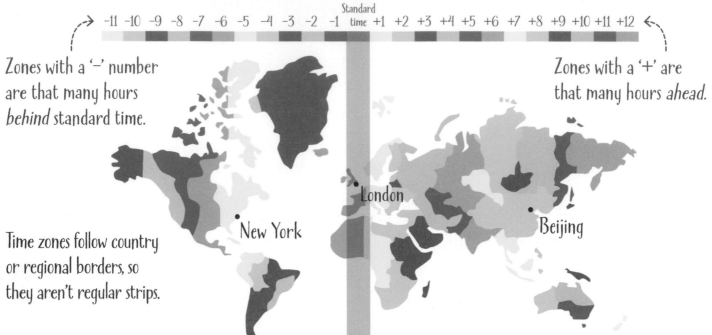

-11 -10 -9 -8 -7 -6 -5 -4 -3 -2 -1 | Standard time | +1 +2 +3 +4 +5 +6 +7 +8 +9 +10 +11 +12

Zones with a '–' number are that many hours *behind* standard time.

Zones with a '+' are that many hours *ahead*.

London

New York

Beijing

Time zones follow country or regional borders, so they aren't regular strips.

If it is 10 a.m. in London, New York is 5 hours behind (5 a.m.) and Beijing is 8 hours ahead (6 p.m.).

This caller is speaking to family in different time zones. Can you work out the time for each?

Standard time: London

15:20

Rome: + 1 hour

____:____

Chicago: – 6 hours

____:____

Can you draw the hands onto the faces of these world clocks?

London, UK
Standard time

Moscow, Russia
+3

Delhi, India
+5 hrs 30

Tunis, Tunisia
+1

Salvador, Brazil
-3

Seattle, USA
-8

The United States is so big, it has several time zones. Starting in the east, each time zone moving west is one hour behind the zone before.

If the time in New York is 12:00, what time is it in...

Houston: ___:___

Jackson: ___:___

San Diego: ___:___

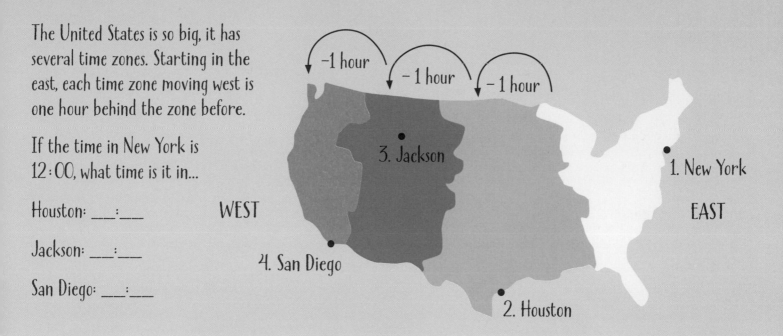

WEST

EAST

3. Jackson

1. New York

4. San Diego

2. Houston

−1 hour   −1 hour   −1 hour

Can you match each ticket with a passenger and fill in the arrival times on the tickets? Arrival times are in local time, so don't forget to add or subtract the time difference when working it out.

Departure: 10 a.m.
Journey time: 6 hours
Time difference: + 3 hours
Arrival: Beijing ___:___

Departure: 6 a.m.
Journey time: 5 hours
Time difference: − 3 hours
Arrival: Lima ___:___

Departure: 8 a.m.
Journey time: 8 hours
Time difference: + 2 hours
Arrival: Rome ___:___

We're arriving at 8 a.m.

We get there at 6 p.m.

I land at at 7 p.m.

Fill in the times on the clocks.

___ : ___   Half past four in the morning

 Ten to seven

___ : ___   Five past eleven in the morning

___ : ___   Quarter to ten in the morning

 1 o'clock

 Twenty past three

Score

___
6

Sticker

Which intervals should be measured in minutes? Circle them.

Building a museum   Toasting bread

Reading every book ever written   Sneezing

Getting dressed   Making a cup of tea

How many did you circle?

....

Can you fill in the blanks?

Journey times		
Start	End	How long it took
8:30	9:00	
13:15		3 hours
	3:30	1 ½ hours

Score

___
6

Sticker

Fill in the times on the clocks, using 24-hour time.

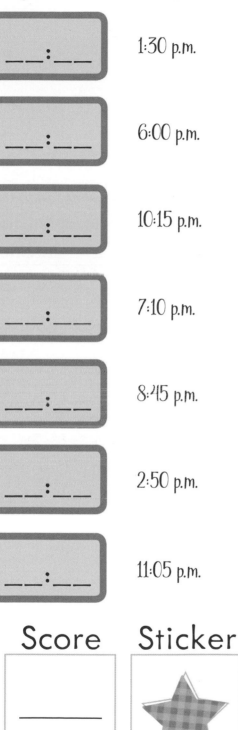

__ __ : __ __   1:30 p.m.

__ __ : __ __   6:00 p.m.

__ __ : __ __   10:15 p.m.

__ __ : __ __   7:10 p.m.

__ __ : __ __   8:45 p.m.

__ __ : __ __   2:50 p.m.

__ __ : __ __   11:05 p.m.

Score
7

Sticker

If it is 1 o'clock in the afternoon standard time, what time is it in these countries?

Standard time   Kenya: +3   Chile: −4

China: +8   Greenland: −2

Can you put these times in order, from early in the day to late, by writing a number in each circle?

◯ 17:10   ◯ 10:30 a.m.

◯ 6 a.m.   ◯ 9:20 p.m.

◯ 12 noon

Score
9

Sticker

Clock workshop

Practise what you've learned so far in this clock workshop.

Can you help repair these clocks?

Can you help put the tools away? Each tool has a label showing how long it was used for. Draw a line to the matching peg.

5 mins   27 mins   1 hr 15 mins   1 hr 20 mins   90 mins

Add a little hand so it shows 4 o'clock.

about half an hour

13:05 – 13:10

11:10 – 12:30

9:15 – 10:30

1 hr 30 mins

Add a big hand so it shows 2:25.

These clocks should all say 11 o'clock in the evening. Can you work out which clock should go in which box?

23:00

22:00

11:00 p.m.

18:45

Ticking along nicely   A

Need fixing   B

Add both hands to this clock so it shows 8:55.

Sometimes, the numbers on a clock are written as Roman numerals.

Can you get these clocks ready by sticking on the right clock face from the sticker pages?

Half past three

8:30

12:30

Half past ten

Can you help finish the clock face, writing the numbers in Roman numerals?

This was the way numbers were written in Ancient Rome.

Modern numbers	Roman numerals
1	I
2	II
3	III
4	IV
5	V
6	VI
7	VII
8	VIII
9	IX
10	X
11	XI
12	XII

Roman numeral tips

V = 5
'V' is like the five fingers of a hand.

X = 10
'X' is like both hands crossed (with 10 fingers).

An 'I' on the left of a number means *minus* 1.

IV 5 − 1 = 4
IX 10 − 1 = 9

An 'I' on the right of a number means *plus* 1.

VII 5 + 2 = 7
VIII 5 + 3 = 8

Football match

The match is made up of two halves. Each half lasts 45 minutes, and there is a fifteen minute break at half-time. Can you fill in the blanks in the timetable?

	Start	End
First half	17:30	
Half-time		
Second half		

The red team is in this goal for the first half. In the second half, it's the blue team. It's 18:35 now. Can you make the goal keeper's shirt the right shade – red or blue?

How long is each player on the pitch for? Write the number of minutes by each one.

Player	On the pitch
1	17:30 – 18:15
2	17:40 – 18:30
3	19:00 – 19:45

How long into the first half was each goal scored? The match started at 17:30.

Goal scored at	Minutes into the match
17:50	
18:00	
18:10	

Can you circle when the team's next games in June will be? The team has one on the first Saturday, on Friday 18th and on the last day of the month.

June						
Mon	Tues	Wed	Thu	Fri	Sat	Sun
	1	2	3	4	5	6
7	8	9	10	11	12	13
14	15	16	17	18	19	20
21	22	23	24	25	26	27
28	29	30				

Can you finish colouring in the picture, following the key?

o'clock   ten past   quarter past   twenty past
half past   twenty to   quarter to   ten to

55

Answers

4-5 On the hour

The inventor's day, from top to bottom:
8 o'clock, 11 o'clock, 2 o'clock and 4 o'clock.

The new clocks, from left to right:
4 o'clock, 10 o'clock and 3 o'clock.

The time machine leaves at 2 o'clock and arrives at 8 o'clock.

6-7 Half past the hour

Fire extinguisher   Jetpack   Invisibility potion

Mind control clocks, from left to right:

The superhero is in Moscow at half past 8, in Mumbai at 10 o'clock and in Sydney at half past 11.

The suspects left the building at:

A: half past one
B: two o'clock
C: three o'clock

Suspect C was the thief.

8-9 More practice

Palm   Creeper   Poppies   Ferns

Cacti

Green house summer times: opens at half past nine, and closes at half past four.

There are 30 minutes until the next Fern Talk.

Greenhouse Quiz:
1. False   2. True   3. False   4. True

10-11 Quarter past and quarter to

Shelf order, from top to bottom: 2nd, 1st, 3rd.

Photo times, from top to bottom: quarter to three, quarter past four and quarter to six.

Musical chairs   Pin the tail   Pass the parcel

12-13 5 minute gaps

Lesson posters, from left to right: ten past four and twenty to five.

Race B is starting now.

The lost watch:

14 More practice

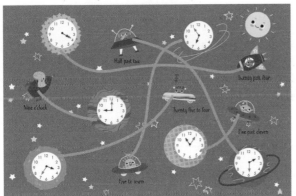

The alien message order:
1. purple 2. yellow 3. orange 4. blue

15–16 Build a clock

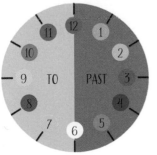

The missing labels, starting from the top and going in a clockwise direction: five past, twenty past, twenty-five past, half past, quarter to, ten to.

17 More practice

The rockets, from left to right: orange, red, blue, green.

The missing times in the story: quarter past eight, quarter past nine, quarter past ten, quarter to four, quarter to five.

18–19 A.M. and P.M.

The bear's day: 1. half past six a.m.
2. ten a.m. 3. quarter past seven p.m.
4. half past ten p.m.

Stick fireflies by these times:
10 p.m. 5 a.m. 12 midnight 8 p.m. 3 a.m.

Shade these butterflies in:
1st row: first and last butterfly
2nd row: first and third butterfly

20–21 Quick quizzes

The times in words, from top to bottom: half past six, four o'clock, ten past one, quarter to nine, twenty-five past seven.

Earlier or later, from top to bottom: later, earlier, earlier, later.

Draw lines between: Midday and 12 noon
11 in the evening and 11 p.m.
Midnight and 12 at night
11 a.m. and 11 in the morning

The times in order:
1. 9 a.m. 2. 11 a.m. 3. 12 midday 4. 3 p.m.
5. 6 p.m. 6. 11 p.m.

22-23 Digital clocks

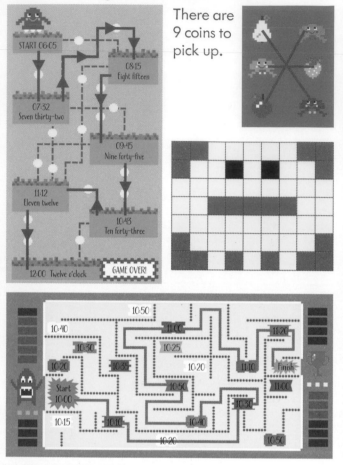

There are 9 coins to pick up.

24-25 More practice

Arrival times in order:
1st: pumpkin   2nd: horse   3rd: dragon

The banquet starts next.

The prince unfreezes at half past eight.
The frog becomes a prince at twenty to ten.

10:30   08:45   11:00

The two times to cross out for Cinderella
are 'Midday' and '12 noon'.

26-27 24-hour time

14:20   14:50   15:00   15:30

These are the stickers to add to the table.

22:45

10:45 p.m.

The spraying hose time: 18:35.

The fire extinguishers, from top to bottom:
05:00 p.m.   07:20 p.m.   09:00 p.m.

The name of the trucks, from left to right: Hero, Roadstar and Champion.

28-29 More practice

The bird saying "ten to three" has got the time wrong.

Scientist's notes:
Iguana: 14:15
Millipede: 17:55
Tree frog: 23:30
Stag beetle: 18:03

Matching leaves:
16:00 and 4 p.m.
13:00 and 1 p.m.
20:00 and 8 p.m.

Times in the key:
7 p.m. = 19:00   4 p.m. = 16:00
8 p.m. = 20:00   6 p.m. = 18:00
1 p.m. = 13:00   11 p.m. = 23:00
3 p.m. = 15:00   10 p.m. = 22:00

The feathers belong to this bird.

30-31 Quick quizzes

03:10	02:30
01:00	11:55
05:50	04:20

1. seven fifteen
2. five to six
3. eleven twenty
4. five past four
5. nine thirty

22:00	08:00 p.m.
18:30	05:15 p.m.
15:55	02:30 p.m.
12:45	11:55 p.m.
20:20	00:10 a.m.
16:30	03:40 p.m.
12:10	04:45 p.m.

32-33 Seconds, minutes, hours

The polar quiz, from top to bottom:
5 seconds, 2 seconds, 7 hours, 5 hours.

The seal on the left should have 2 fish and the seal on the right should have 6 fish.

The polar explorer takes 1 hour 5 minutes to get ready.

The husky racer finishes in 1 hour 50 minutes, so she succeeds.

34-35 How long?

The red turtle took 10 mins.
The green turtle took 20 mins.
So the green turtle ate for longer.

The puppy events lasted for 1 hour 15 mins.

Grooming: 30 mins   Competing: 30 mins
Prizegiving: 15 mins

Catch the mouse was the longest event.

The parrot's journey home took 2 hrs 10 mins.
The goat's journey took 2 hrs 5 mins.
So the parrot's journey was the longest.

36-37 Start and end times

The helicopter rides, from top to bottom:
13:50, 14:20, 14:50.

The green jet drops a parachutist at the 5th green spot. The red jet drops one at the last red spot.

The pilot on the left took off at 13:45.
The pilot on the right took off at 14:15.

38–39 More practice

The 1st popcorn batch took 1 min 40 seconds and the 2nd took 2 mins 30 seconds.

The journey takes 28 minutes, so you would arrive in time for the film.

The Inventor has the longest running time.

From left to right, the films last for: 90, 120 and 150 minutes.

The film ends at 19:30.

40–41 Days, weeks, months

Add a pirate flag to the ship on the right.

It will take 21 days or 3 weeks to reach Treasure Island.

Put a cross on square D7.

42–43 Counting years

The squirrels' ages, from left to right: 5, 10, 13.

It is 12 weeks until the deer's first birthday.
52 − 40 = 12

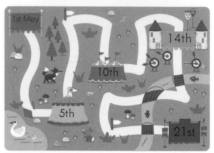

44–45 Quick quizzes

days	21 days
week	15 minutes
minute	2 years
days	120 seconds
minutes	2 weeks
hour	2 hours
months	90 minutes
day	1 ½ minutes
weeks	½ an hour
	3 minutes

1. The journey ends at 5:30.
2. The journey starts at 9:30.
3. The journey takes 1½ hours.

Start	End	How long
9:00	9:30	30 mins
4:30	5:45	1 hr 15
1:30	2:00	30 mins
11:15	13:15	2 hrs
16:50	17:20	30 mins
18:45	19:45	1 hr

46–77 How time works

Photos around the world:
1. Daytime photo 2. Sunset photo
3. Nighttime photo

Matching turns:
24 hours = 1 turn   12 hours = ½ turn

It is 360 days until the next birthday.

True or false:
1. True 2. False 3. False 4. True

Next leap
year parties:
2020
2024
2028

48–49 Time zones

In Rome the time is 16:20.
In Chicago the time is 9:20.

In Houston it is 11:00, in Jackson it is 10:00
and in San Diego it is 9:00.

Arrival times on tickets:
Beijing: 7 p.m.   Lima: 8 a.m.   Rome: 6 p.m.

50–51 Quick quizzes

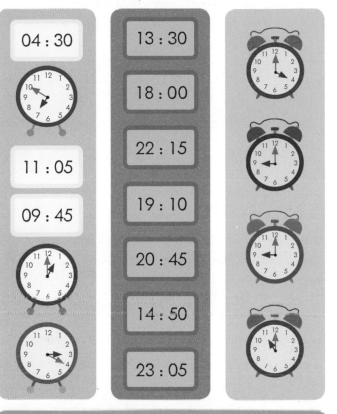

04 : 30	13 : 30
11 : 05	18 : 00
09 : 45	22 : 15
	19 : 10
	20 : 45
	14 : 50
	23 : 05

There are 3 intervals to circle: getting dressed, making toast, making a cup of tea.

Start	End	How long
8:30	9:00	30 mins
13:15	16:15	3 hrs
2:00	3:30	1 ½ hrs

Times in order:
1. 6 a.m.   2. 10:30 a.m.   3. 12 noon
4. 17:10   5. 9:20 p.m.

52–53 Clock workshop

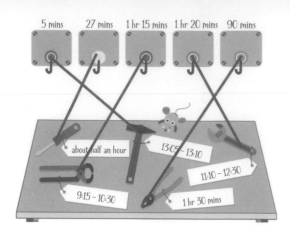

5 mins · 27 mins · 1 hr 15 mins · 1 hr 20 mins · 90 mins

about half an hour · 13:05 – 13:10 · 11:10 – 12:30 · 9:15 – 10:30 · 1 hr 30 mins

The purple and blue clock go in box B. The rest go in box A.

The players are on the pitch, from left to right: 45, 50 and 45 minutes.

From top to bottom, the goals were scored 20, 30 and 40 minutes into the match.

June

Mon	Tues	Wed	Thu	Fri	Sat	Sun
	1	2	3	4	5	6
7	8	9	10	11	12	13
14	15	16	17	18	19	20
21	22	23	24	25	26	27
28	29	30				

56-57 Road trip

54-55 Football match

	Start	End
1st Half	17:30	18:15
Half-time	18:15	18:30
2nd Half	18:30	19:15

Shade the goalkeeper's shirt blue.

Edited by Rosie Dickins   Managing designer: Zoe Wray

First published in 2017 by Usborne Publishing Ltd., 83-85 Saffron Hill, London, EC1N 8RT, England. www.usborne.com Copyright © 2017 Usborne Publishing Ltd.